Scriptures taken from the HOLY BIBLE, NEW LIVING TRANSLATION, Copyright © 1996, 2004, 2007 by Tynsdale House Foundation. Used by permission of Tynsdale House Publishers, Inc., Carol Stream, Illinois 60188. All rights reserved. Used by permission.

E.R. Violet Publishing, LLC
West Des Moines, IA 50266
violetpublish@gmail.com

Printed in the United States of America

Illustrations by Bill Love

Book Design by WORD**ART**, West Des Moines, IA

This book belongs to

_____

(A child of God)

Pastor Pickle

and the

Criss-Cross Signal

Bill & Lona Love

One warm Saturday morning, Pastor Percy Pickle and his dog, Doogie, were walking in Pioneer Park when he saw a group of children huddled in a circle on the playground.

As he got closer, Pastor Pickle saw two young girls in the middle, yelling at each other. The other kids were shouting, too. As the argument continued to heat up, the girls began shoving each other and calling each other names.

Pastor Pickle recognized one of the girls and called out to her. "Lilly Lavender!" he shouted, and all the children stopped yelling and turned to see him walking toward the group. "What seems to be the trouble here?"

Doogie watched as all the other children except Lilly Lavender ran off in different directions.

"What was all the yelling about?" asked Pastor Pickle.

"That was Marci Moon!" said Lilly Lavender. "She doesn't like me and I don't like her, either. We never seem to agree on anything and we usually end up arguing and yelling at each other. Like just now! There's just so much drama with her! She called me stupid and ugly and thinks I'm wrong about everything. I think she just likes to fight. Or at least she likes to pick fights with me!"

"I see," said Pastor Pickle. "And how do you usually handle the situation?"

"At first, I just turned my back and ignored her," answered Lilly Lavender. "Then one day, I heard her and her friends laughing at me. I got real mad and began yelling back at her."

"Why, Lilly Lavender! I'm surprised at your response," said Pastor Pickle.

"I didn't know what else to do!" said Lilly Lavender with a sad look on her face. "I can't let her push me around all the time, especially in front of my friends."

"Well, first of all, you're not stupid, ugly or wrong all the time. Those are just hurtful things said to make you feel bad. But there's a better way to handle situations such as this," said Pastor Pickle. "How about if you walk back toward the church with Doogie and me and we can talk more about it?"

As they walked along the path, Pastor Pickle continued, "You know, the Bible clearly spells out two very important commandments we are all to follow. Love God and love each other. They're really very simple."

"Well, I do love God," said Lilly Lavender. "But I don't think I could ever love Marci Moon."

Pastor Pickle smiled at Lilly Lavender. "God doesn't say that we should love everyone *except* those we don't particularly like. He says we are to love *all* others as we love ourselves."

"Does that mean I have to hug and kiss Marci Moon like I do my grandmother?" asked Lilly Lavender with a scrunched up nose. "Ew, ick!"

"No, that's not what God means," explained Pastor Pickle. "He means for us to see others in the same way he sees them. We are all his children and he loves each and every one of us. When he commands us to love one another, he doesn't mean the kind of love we think of between a boy and a girl, or even family members. The love he commands means we are to treat each other with respect. We are to be patient and tolerant of each other and not over-react in situations where we might not agree. Our relationships with others should always be helpful, not hurtful."

As Pastor Pickle and Lilly Lavender approached the church, the next door neighbor, Norbert Notch, came rushing across the yard toward them. He looked angry and started waving his arms at Pastor Pickle as he got closer.

"Pastor Pickle, I've just about had it with all these noisy kids you always have running around here!" Norbert Notch shouted.

"Norbert Notch!" said Pastor Pickle, with a smile on his face. "Good to see you here, neighbor." Gesturing toward the church, he said, "Come in. Our church secretary, Stella Stencil, has made some very good lemonade."

"I'm not here for pleasantries," Norbert Notch growled.

"You see that fence over there?" he asked, pointing toward the large privacy fence running between his back yard and the church yard. "I built that fence specifically to keep these kids and their various balls, frisbees and other playthings out of my yard. I take great pride in keeping my yard and bushes and flowers looking perfect at all times. It's bad enough that I have to listen to these kids screaming and laughing and yelling all the time! I won't have them ruining my yard, too!"

"Well, that fence certainly should do the job," replied Pastor Pickle, looking patiently at Norbert Notch.

"You would think so," continued Norbert Notch, turning red in the face. "But no! Balls and frisbees still sail over the fence all the time. Then come the kids, climbing up and over the fence to retrieve their stuff. I just want them to quiet down and stay out of my yard! My fence is getting beat up, my wife's beautiful flowers have been stepped on and my grass is getting trampled. I've had it! I'm out of patience!"

Taking a step closer to Pastor Pickle, Norbert Notch shouted, "I want you to put a stop to all this! And I mean right now!"

Pastor Pickle took a deep breath and said in a calm voice, "I'm very sorry. I'll have a talk with the kids that play in our church yard about respecting your property and your wishes."

"I hope you do!" snarled Norbert Notch as he turned and headed for his house.

"Good to see you, Norbert Notch." Pastor Pickle called to his neighbor. "Please join us at church sometime. We'd like to get to know you better."

"Don't hold your breath!" mumbled Norbert Notch as he rounded the fence to his yard.

Pastor Pickle and Lilly Lavender stood in silence for a moment, looking toward Norbert Notch's house.

"Whew!" said Lilly Lavender, finally. "You have your own Marci Moon, don't you?"

Pastor Pickle nodded as he put his hand on Lilly Lavender's shoulder.

"Well, there's no shortage of people in this world who, for one reason or another, are not very happy," said Pastor Pickle. "And when we're not happy, it's easy for us to forget about the commandment to love one another. Norbert Notch has become a very lonely man since his wife died last year. I'm sure he's still mourning her loss. That's no excuse for losing his temper with me, but things build up in his mind and he needs to let off steam to someone. I guess I'm handy, being right next door."

"Can I ask you something?" said Lilly Lavender. "While Norbert Notch was yelling at you, I noticed you holding your hand behind your back with your fingers crossed. What was that all about?"

"Well, I call that my criss-cross signal," explained Pastor Pickle. "Whenever I find myself in difficult situations where I may be tempted to over-react and do or say something that would be hurtful rather than helpful, I use my criss-cross signal to remind myself of the cross sitting on the top of our church steeple."

Lilly Lavender looked up at the cross as Pastor Pickle continued, "I try to be kind, respectful and patient with everyone I see and talk to throughout the day, but sometimes, in situations like the one you just saw, I may need a reminder to control my thoughts and my tongue. So I give myself a signal to remember the cross and the love it represents by crossing my fingers. Then I take a deep breath and try to respond to the other person in love instead of in anger."

"So this is your criss-cross signal?" asked Lilly Lavender, putting her hand behind her back and crossing her first two fingers.

"It is," said Pastor Pickle. "And you might want to try using it to remind yourself of the cross the next time you start to react to someone in anger rather than love."

That afternoon, when Lilly Lavender arrived home and went to her bedroom at the top of the stairs, her mother, Loretta Lavender, was waiting for her.

"Lilly Lavender, how many times do I have to tell you to clean up your room and make your bed? You should be ashamed of how it looks! Before you even think about doing anything else, I want this mess cleaned up! Do you understand me?"

Lilly Lavender's first reaction was to get mad at her mother and blurt out all the reasons she could think of for why she shouldn't have to bother with her room right now. But just as she started to open her mouth, she remembered her conversation with Pastor Pickle about the criss-cross signal. So, she crossed her fingers, took a deep breath and calmly said, "I'm sorry, Mom. I guess I was just in a hurry to get to the playground this morning. I'll clean my room and make my bed right now."

Loretta Lavender looked at her daughter in surprise. Then a big smile spread across her face.

"Thank you, sweetheart," she said to Lilly Lavender, walking over to her and giving her a big hug. "I'm so proud of you when you act this way! This is the sweet daughter I love."

Lilly Lavender cleaned up her room and made her bed, thinking all the while that Pastor Pickle's criss-cross signal had resulted in happiness for both her and her mother.

After church the next Sunday, Lilly Lavender told Pastor Pickle the story about using the criss-cross signal with her mother and how it changed what could have been a harsh argument into smiles and hugs.

"That's great!" said Pastor Pickle. "You know, respect is a big part of the love God asks us to show to one another. In the Bible, he instructs us to honor our fathers and mothers. You obeyed that command by showing your mother a great deal of love and respect when you responded to her the way you did. And she loved you back. Isn't that what loving one another is all about?"

"From now on," Lilly Lavender said excitedly, "I'm going to try to remember to use the criss-cross signal more often."

A few days later, Lilly Lavender and her friends were at the playground, when she heard laughing behind her. She turned to see Marci Moon and her friends approaching, pointing in her direction and snickering to each other.

"Lilly Lavender!" snarled Marci Moon as she reached the group at the teeter-totter. "Move out of our way. We want to use the teeter-totter for a while."

"But we just got here and we're just getting started," replied Lilly Lavender, feeling the anger start to build up and bracing herself for the fight she knew was coming.

"I don't really care," said Marci Moon with a cross look on her face. "You don't own the teeter-totter and we want to use it now, so go find something else to do."

Lilly Lavender opened her mouth to angrily respond to Marci Moon, when she remembered the criss-cross signal and what a difference it had made in the conversation with her mother. So, instead of clenching her fists at her side, she crossed her fingers and took a deep breath before she spoke.

"Marci Moon, you can have a turn," said Lilly Lavender, motioning to the other end of the teeter-totter, "because I've been wanting to ask you about something, anyway."

"What do you want to know?" asked Marci Moon, curious as to why Lilly Lavender was so willing to share the teeter-totter with her.

"Well," said Lilly Lavender, "I think you always wear the coolest outfits of anyone in our school. I love the colors you choose and they always match perfectly. I wanted to ask if your mother picks them out for you or if you choose them yourself?"

Marci Moon looked down at what she was wearing.

"Uh, it depends," she said, with a puzzled look on her face, wondering what Lilly Lavender was up to. "Sometimes I choose them. Sometimes my mom chooses them."

"I just really like the way you dress and I thought I should tell you about it," replied Lilly Lavender.

"Really?" asked Marci Moon, a cautious smile beginning to appear on her face as they continued to go up and down on the teeter-totter.

"Actually, my mom is the one with the good taste," Marci Moon said after a while. "She picks out most of my clothes. I think if she left it to me I'd probably look like I picked them out wearing a blindfold."

They both laughed and so did all their friends.

Lilly Lavender smiled and uncrossed her fingers.

The next day, Pastor Pickle looked out his office window and saw Norbert Notch on a ladder, pounding nails to add extensions to the top of his fence, making it even taller.

Pastor Pickle closed his eyes, and began a silent prayer:

Lord, please soften Norbert Notch's heart. Teach him about your love and the meaning of spreading that love to others. Teach him patience and tolerance. And Lord, please give him some companionship to relieve his loneliness.

Just as Pastor Pickle opened his eyes again, he heard Norbert Notch yell out and saw the ladder fall from beneath him as he tumbled to the ground.

Pastor Pickle ran out the front door of the church and across the church yard to where Norbert Notch was lying flat on his back, moaning.

"Norbert Notch!" cried Pastor Pickle as he bent over his neighbor, who was obviously in pain. "Are you okay?"

"Does it look like I'm okay?" groaned Norbert Notch, with a pained, angry look on his face.

"I'll go call for help," said Pastor Pickle.

"No, don't call anybody," snapped Norbert Notch. "Just help me up. I'll be okay."

But Pastor Pickle could see that Norbert Notch was hurting more than he was letting on.

"I'm going to get my car and take you to the hospital," said Pastor Pickle. "You've obviously hurt yourself more than you think."

And he had.

When they returned from the emergency room a few hours later, Norbert Notch had a cast on his broken leg and was walking with the help of crutches.

Several times a day for the next two weeks, Pastor Pickle went next door to check on Norbert Notch. Pastor Pickle's wife, Pearl Pickle, and other families from the church also made and delivered meals for him, staying to visit for a few minutes each time.

One day during his morning walk, Pastor Pickle saw Lilly Lavender, Marci Moon and their friends having fun together on the playground in Pioneer Park. He smiled to himself as he saw how the two former enemies were getting along so well and seemed to have become friends.

"Lilly Lavender!" Pastor Pickle called out as he approached the group. "May I have a word with you and your friends?"

The kids stopped playing and gathered around Pastor Pickle, who told them of a plan he had and asked if they would be willing to help.

The next Saturday, just as Norbert Notch was finishing the breakfast Pearl Pickle had brought to his door that morning, he heard a lot of voices outside.

"Those darn kids!" he thought to himself. "They're in my yard again."

He grabbed his crutches and limped toward the window. What he saw outside surprised him. Almost a dozen kids were walking around his yard with tools in their hands as Pastor Pickle directed them to various tasks.

Lilly Lavender and Marci Moon laughed as they pulled weeds in the flower bed. Henry Hardy, the church handyman, mowed the lawn. Trey Tinker and Jade Jolley raked the dead grass behind the mower. Zoey Zingerman swept the walkways, while Scarlett and Sadie Saddle picked up dead branches and twigs and put them in recycle bags. Elsie Edge helped Kaiya Kronk water the bushes. And Eli Eggers and Teegan Teaberry were carrying the filled recycle bags to the curb.

Norbert Notch couldn't believe his eyes! He plopped down in his chair by the large picture window and watched the kids work until all the tasks were finished and his yard looked perfect. Then the kids took all the tools back to the church shed, where Pastor Pickle thanked them and said a short prayer.

The next day, as Pastor Pickle was watching the sanctuary fill with people for the Sunday morning service, he was surprised to see Norbert Notch hobble in on crutches and sit down in one of the back pews.

Pastor Pickle's sermon was about loving God and loving each other and what a difference that can make in our lives.

When the service was over, Norbert Notch was one of the last to leave. He stopped to talk to Pastor Pickle at the door.

"Will you thank those kids for me?" said Norbert Notch with a frown on his face. "I would have said something to them, but they disappeared too fast when they were finished."

"Thank them yourself," said Pastor Pickle with a smile. "We're going to be roasting hot dogs Thursday evening at the fire pit behind the church. Why don't you join us and meet the kids? They would enjoy that!"

"Nah," Norbert Notch said, scowling. "You thank them for me." And before Pastor Pickle could respond, Norbert Notch had turned and started home.

That Thursday evening, Pastor Pickle, Pearl Pickle, the kids who had helped in Norbert Notch's yard, and some of the adults from the church who had been taking meals to Norbert Notch, gathered at the fire pit. They roasted hot dogs and marshmallows and had a fun meal.

When they were nearly finished, Pastor Pickle looked up and saw Norbert Notch making his way on crutches across the yard toward them. The group fell silent as Norbert Notch approached. Had they been making too much noise?

"Norbert Notch!" called Pastor Pickle. "What brings you out on this beautiful evening?" asked Pastor Pickle.

"I've got a few things I need to get off my chest," said Norbert Notch. He looked around at the group of children and adults who were now looking back at him attentively.

"I've been yelling at you kids for a long time now to quiet down and quit jumping my fence and stay out of my yard. When that didn't do any good, I came over here and gave Pastor Pickle a piece of my mind."

Lilly Lavender remembered that episode well! Everyone was bracing for what they thought was coming next.

"I guess I'm just too old to remember what it's like to be young and have as much energy as you have," Norbert Notch continued. "But then I sat at my window last Saturday and watched you people use that energy to mow my grass and clean up my yard. Then, on Sunday, I heard Pastor Pickle speak about God's love and how we should learn what it means to share that love with one another. I've been doing a lot of thinking about it since."

"I know I need to practice what Pastor Pickle preaches," Norbert Notch said with a grin starting to form on his face. "So, to you grownups, I want to say 'thank you' for bringing me meals and running errands for me and everything else you've done to help me while I've been laid up. I realize now that I witnessed God's love through you."

Then looking at the kids, Norbert Notch said, "And to you noisy, energetic bunch of kids, I want to say 'thank you,' and apologize for being so intolerant and cranky toward you. I've seen a wonderful, unselfish group of God's children sharing God's love with me these last few weeks!"

By this time, everyone was looking around at each other in amazement.

"Because you're such generous people," Norbert Notch concluded, "I have one more favor to ask."

Norbert Notch turned to Pastor Pickle and said, "This Saturday, could these kids use some of the church's tools and come over to my yard and help me tear down that darn fence?"

Everyone was stunned! Had they heard correctly? Did Norbert Notch really want to take down his fence?

All the kids began to rush toward him, introducing themselves, shaking his hand and giving him hugs. Norbert Notch was overwhelmed with emotion at all the attention.

Lilly Lavender looked around and caught Pastor Pickle's eye. She gave him a big smile and flashed the criss-cross signal to him.

Smiling back at Lilly Lavender,
Pastor Pickle crossed his fingers, too,
as they both looked up at the cross
on the top of the steeple.

A Message From Pastor Pickle

Many times every day, we're presented with a choice for how we respond in certain anger-filled situations. We can choose to react with more anger or we can choose to respond with a measure of God's love.

How do you usually react when someone says something that makes you mad? Do you choose to show God's love or do you make matters worse by responding in a hurtful way?

We have many opportunities to show God's love to those around us through patience and tolerance, through respect and understanding, and by being helpful rather than hurtful. And that's exactly what God wants us to do.

In fact, that's what he commands us to do. The Bible says, "anyone who does not love does not know God, for God is love."

So, the next time someone's attitude toward you makes you angry, try taking a deep breath and use my criss-cross signal to remind yourself of God's unconditional love. And then pass that same love along to the person you're dealing with.

Say this prayer with me:

Dear God

Thank you for loving me. Help me to share your love with all those around me by always being respectful, showing patience and understanding in difficult situations, and responding in helpful rather than in hurtful ways. It's always for your glory that I pray these things.

Amen

Additional References

This is my command: Love each other.
John 15:17 (NLT)

Always be humble and gentle. Be patient with each other, making allowance for each other's faults because of your love.
1 Ephesians 4:2 (NLT)

Don't just pretend to love others. Really love them.
Romans 12:9 (NLT)

You have heard the law that says, 'Love your neighbor' and hate your enemy. But I say love your enemies! Pray for those who persecute you! In that way you will be acting as true children of your Father in heaven.
Matthew 5:43-45 (NLT)

But anyone who does not love does not know God, for God is love.
1 John 4:8 (NLT)

84537194R00033

Made in the USA
Lexington, KY
22 March 2018